CW01091515

ALEJANDRO PATTERSON & SIMON HILTON

Product Strategy Bridge

First edition

This book was professionally typeset on Reedsy.
Find out more at reedsy.com

Contents

V   The Framework

VI   Write it down, and share it

VII   Conclusion

I

Introduction

1

The Slack Message

We began the journey of writing this book when Alejandro and I met at a scaling SAAS company. We had multiple products in multiple markets and it was our role to make sure we had the people, process, and tools to move teams towards our goals.

Alejandro had joined to lead our innovation stream and so needed to get a high-level overview of our intentions across all streams. After completing a tour of the organization he reached out to me on Slack and asked

"Hey Simon, can we please book in some time to talk about our road maps?"

My reply was simple

"Sure, but at the same time, can we please talk about strategy?"

Alejandro replied with a winky face emoji and at that point we both understood. We did not have a problem developing a delivery plan. The teams were busy working away on building features but none of us could draw a straight line to why this mattered and how it would impact our business goals.

From our first meeting, it was clear that our task was not

in making more road maps but developing a way to connect business goals with team activities that clearly communicated the teams direction and the direction of the product.

Alejandro had approached these same problems during his time at a large insurer. What he realised in a light bulb moment was that the process he was working with was rigid, and was lacking any agile methodology. To improve this he focussed more on

- Product goals and strategies and the measures to guide decision making
- Developing room for testing, experimentation or leveraging data

This connection of business strategy, product strategy and team development resonated with many of the stakeholders as they could for the first time see how work at the team level layered up and contributed to the business goals.

We have continued to use these methods in other organisations. After sharing this with colleagues and talking with other product and executive leaders, we saw many of the same problems; no shared understanding, no common language, and no clear direction which leads to confusion across the organisation.

We wrote this playbook to help any product team create alignment with their business, earn confidence with their business leaders and ultimately take on more accountability for their work.

2

How To Use This Book

First, thank you for taking the time to read this book. Often product teams are overstretched and so busy working on urgent issues that the important work is not done. And strategy is important, especially as a product leader. Every decision of what to work on is literally worth hundreds of thousands, if not millions, of dollars. Development teams are expensive so shipping and maintaining features for your customers has an impact across your organization.

Effectively communicating your direction and gaining the confidence of your stakeholders is critical to working on the right outcomes and having the support to get them to market as well as inviting guidance from different perspectives.

We wrote this book expecting you to read it from start to finish. We deliberately kept it small, so it is a practical play book that you can read and share with your team. Our focus is on product strategy, and while business strategy is a part of that, those looking for an in depth understanding of business strategy should probably try elsewhere.

There are a few key roles in a digital product business that we have considered when researching and writing this book:

- If you are a product leader, we focused this book on you and your duty to connect the intention of the business with something that is desirable for customers. You will work with your executive and product teams on tradeoff decisions and use your strategy to align messaging across the company as your representative to push decision making closer to the product teams.
- If you are an executive who lacks confidence in your product teams and their direction, share this book with your product leaders and ask if this is a way you can communicate and align on product direction for your business. Many executives we have spoken to would love to receive such a concise and clear summary from their product leaders, and be updated regularly.
- Finally, if you are a product team member, who lacks clarity in how your work drives any sort of impact or connection to the business, then start writing this yourself and share with your product leader to see if you can fill in the gaps together.

We broke this book up into some key areas to help you understand the relationships and dynamics that go into not only writing, but living a product strategy.

- In The Problem, we will learn about the actual effects that little or no strategy has on the business but also on the people that make it up.

- In The Mindset, we will learn how to move away from a monolithic know it all approach to strategy and how to be more curious and agile.
- In Discovery, we will find out how your strategy is showing up in the market, even if you never intended it to.
- In The Framework, we get into the detail of exactly how you will develop your strategy and its parts.

As you move through the different sections of creating your product strategy, you will most likely find that you will see gaps along the way. For example, when you are trying to answer where you will compete, you may realise you have never done a competitor analysis before. This is ok and expected. Most of the value of this work recognises your gaps and leaning into them rather than ignoring them and continuing with assumptions that don't apply.

It won't be perfect the first time around but we encourage you to get to your first version as soon as possible, recognise your gaps and improve from there.

You can do this.

Let's Begin.

II

The Problem

3

What Is Strategy?

One reason for writing this book is the experience of seeing too many situations where a business strategy is handed to the team but it is not thought out, structured or delivered in a way that is practical for them to use in their day-to-day decision making. This is usually because what is presented as a strategy is a loose set of aspirational statements with no grounding in the current context or worse, a list of features that the team should just get on and deliver. Without this, the team risks focusing on the wrong investments of their time that will not serve the market nor the business, burning through valuable time and money while competitors seize the opportunity.

This behaviour comes from confusion about what a strategy is and how it connects teams. Before we get into what a strategy is, let's eliminate a few things of what a strategy is not.

Product Strategy is not a vision - While a vision is important and aspirational, giving you an idea of what horizons you are shooting for, it doesn't provide enough connection to the current state of the business and therefore no practical guidance to the product team.

Product Strategy is not a business strategy - Business strategies must be developed separately as they need to consider much more financial and legal questions like

- "Why does this company exist?",
- "What do investors want?",
- "How much funding will we need?".

This is important because it provides constraints to operate in and focus on the product team.

Product Strategy is not a delivery plan - Sometimes roadmaps with a set of features to deliver are also substituted for a strategy and while this will generate action it doesn't help teams consider "What impact will this have on our business and our customer", "Why are we building this?" or "Why this and not that?"

Product Strategy is not software- There are many Saas companies claiming that using their software is the path to strategic excellence and they may be right for the monitoring of your operations against the strategy, but they are no substitute for the work of building the strategy. For this, you will only need the tools you commonly use for problem solving like whiteboards or wikis. You may decide to use one of these solutions in the future, but for the initial phase of developing your strategy, they are not required.

So what is a good product strategy, then? After seeing so many complex strategy models that are hard for most of the team to understand, we were drawn to the work of A.G. Lafley, former CEO of Procter & Gamble, and Roger Martin, dean of the Rotman School of Management. In their book "Playing to Win: How Strategy Really Works" they outline five interrelated questions.

1. What is your winning aspiration?
2. *The purpose of your enterprise, it's motivating aspiration.*
3. Where will you play?
4. *A playing field where you can achieve that aspiration.*
5. How will you win?
6. *The way you will win on the chosen playing field.*
7. What capabilities must be in place?
8. *The set and configuration of capabilities required to win in the chosen way.*

13

9. What management systems are required?
10. *The systems and measures that enable the capabilities and support the choices.*

It may seem funny that we are referring to a business strategy book for our product strategy but the way you answer the questions changes when you are focusing on how to develop a product rather than how to develop a business.

This model provides the key elements product teams need to understand their focus and direction, yet is simple enough for anyone to follow. It can take the form of a short conversation, a page on your wiki or even a slide deck so it is portable and malleable enough to fit different audiences. It also provides a great foundation to bring together the activities and choices from various levels of your organisation and tell a coherent story about where you are going.

4

The Effects of Strategy

Bad strategy or not even having a strategy has a leveraged negative effect on your organisation, your teams and customers. It means wasted money from shipping things you shouldn't, lack of confidence from your leaders but most of all it affects the way people feel about working for your organisation.

While researching this book, we talked to dozens of product managers, product leaders, and executives at different sized companies but still found common experiences between them. We found several major themes popping up about how strategy shows up in product teams today.

The first major theme we found was that teams could not connect what they were doing day to day with how it affected the business. Because of this reason, there were other factors at play when deciding what outcomes to pursue. Sometimes it was just what the highest paid person (HiPPO) told them to do and sometimes it was continuing to invest in features that no one could prove was really of value to customers. The outcome was the same. The teams building it could not draw a straight line between what they were doing and how it progressed the business goals. They were confident that a lot of money and time was being wasted on things that really didn't matter for the customer or for the business.

The next major theme was in the relationship between product leaders and executives. Many leaders felt frustrated in not being able to develop effective communication with their executive teams. Attempts at communication were difficult because they could not write in a way that was easy for executives to understand while retaining the important choices that product teams had made. Documents either took an executive or product focus instead of developing a format that bridged the two and could be reused across the org.

Finally, we found that there was quite a profound and recurring point that the lack of direction present in teams was a clear demotivator and has led many to leave the organisation they were working for. This is probably the most startling point we can make. If you want to retain more staff, especially top performers, then it is critical you give them an understanding of where you are going, why it matters and the space to explore what will create impact. This gives them the context to inspire their intrinsic motivation and figure out a way to get there.

Having this kind of strategy empowers teams to decide when leaders aren't in the room and pushes those decisions closer to teams and checking their decisions with "How does this align to the strategy". This document also serves as a guidance to the larger organisation, so when someone comes to your team with the next most amazing idea from a customer they need to close, they can easily test whether the idea is on or off strategy.

III

The Mindset

5

Trust but Verify

Context, confidence and language

Trust is a vital component of successful teams and organisations. It allows for open communication, cooperation and collaboration, which in turn leads to high-performing teams and effective decision-making. Without trust, teams and organisations can become siloed and bogged down by internal competition and lack of cooperation, leading to costly and ineffective outcomes.

A strategic approach to building trust and alignment within an organisation is essential for creating a culture of trust and cooperation. By clearly defining and communicating the organisation's goals and objectives, and regularly revisiting and updating them, teams can work towards a shared purpose and vision.

To connect your product strategy to the overall business strategy, it is important to first understand the context and drivers behind the business strategy. Trust is built through consistent working relationships over time. To build trust with your team; you need to understand what's on your executive's mind and help achieve those goals. Meet with the executives responsible for the strategy and gather information on its purpose, language, initiatives and goals. Understand how the strategy is translated and interpreted by different stakeholders, and take note of the language, metrics and orientation used.

After this, summarise your findings and share them with your colleagues to refine your understanding and build a narrative that will be essential in communicating and socialising your product strategy. This process will help to build trust and alignment across all levels of the organisation, leading to a more cohesive, high-performing team.

Alignment & Data

When it comes to developing and launching a successful product, it is crucial that all stakeholders are aligned and that progress is regularly measured to minimise waste and keep all teams focussed on customer value.. Alignment and measurement are critical components of a successful product strategy, as they ensure that all teams are working towards the same goals and that progress is tracked using data-driven decisions. When we work in an organisation, there are conventional truths built up over time. Through personal experiences, external triggers, or feedback from customers.

Over time, opinions will proliferate without much data to support these ideas. Data brings back objectivity. Using data will help you dispel all company myths and create alignment on grounded truths

Alignment is essential for ensuring that the product vision and strategy align with the overall company vision and strategy, as well as aligning the product team with other teams within the organisation. This helps to ensure that all teams are working towards the same goals, which is crucial for the success of the product.

For example, if the product team is focused on developing a product that is technically advanced, but the sales team is focused on developing a product that is easy to sell, there will be a disconnect between the two teams. This can lead to a product that is not well-received by the target audience or that does not achieve the desired business outcomes.

Measurement, on the other hand, allows for the tracking of progress and the identification of areas for improvement. By regularly measuring the performance of the product and comparing it to the goals and objectives set out in the product strategy, the product team can make data-driven decisions and adjust the product vision and strategy as needed.

For example, if the product team is regularly measuring customer satisfaction and finds that the product is not meeting the needs of the target audience, they can adjust the product vision and strategy to better meet those needs. This can lead to a more successful product launch, as well as a higher likelihood of product-market fit.

Alignment and measurement also help in understanding the target audience and the market, which leads to better product positioning and pricing strategy. By regularly measuring the performance of the product, the product team can identify areas where the product is performing well and areas where it is not. This can help to inform the product positioning and pricing strategy, which can lead to better ROI and customer acquisition.

6

Make It Testable

As outlined in the previous section, "Alignment and Data," the use of opportunities is an effective method for measuring the success of your product strategy. However, to truly de-risk these opportunities, it's important to implement a structured approach to testing and experimentation.

In product development, testing and experimentation are often overlooked or underutilised. This can lead to those responsible for testing and experimentation feeling unsupported and unskilled. However, testing and experimentation play a crucial role in a successful product strategy. They provide valuable data to validate assumptions and make informed decisions about the direction of your product.

It is important to understand the value of the work that you and your team are delivering by progressively validating the opportunities through testing. Without this understanding, it becomes difficult to adjust your strategy to take advantage of what is working and stop doing what is not working.

Consider this fictitious scenario where you are a product leader at Juicero and the CEO asks you to build a high-end, connected juice press that uses pre-packaged fruits and vegetables to provide fresh juice on demand. The CEO has seen similar products succeed in other industries and believes that there is a market for this type of product, and he has raised over 120m to do so!

You work tirelessly with your product teams to prioritise building the juice press, and you have to de-prioritise some other features to do this work (which you have already validated). Of course it's delivered on time, in scope, and everyone celebrates.

At the end of the quarter, the CEO asks how the juice press is performing. When you analyse the data, you find that the product is not performing as expected. The high cost of the machine and juice packs, as well as the revelation that the juice packs could be squeezed by hand, has made it unappealing to most customers.

In this scenario, it's clear that building the juice press was not aligned with the market, and that although the idea had a huge amount of investment behind it, there was not a clear strategy.

If you had been able to say no to the CEO and used market research and data to back you up, the company could have avoided investing significant resources into a product that ultimately failed. By having a clear strategy and criteria for evaluating new product ideas, you can prioritise initiatives that align with the company's goals and have a better chance of success.

A successful product strategy involves identifying problems and opportunities, placing small bets, testing and learning, and using data to inform decision-making. By generating data through research, tests, and experiments, product teams can validate assumptions, make informed decisions and adjust their strategy accordingly. This approach allows teams to remove strategies that are not serving their business and double down on those that are, while having the data to explain why.

CEO's operate at a business strategy level but that would need to be intrinsically connected to your product strategy. The first question you should be able to ask is "sure, we can do that, can you help me understand how this is connected to our strategy?".

The process for testing and experimentation can be broken down into several practical steps:

- **Define the problem or opportunity:** Clearly define and size the problem or opportunity that you are trying to solve or capitalise on. This will serve as the basis for your bet and help to guide your testing and experimentation.
- **Develop a hypothesis**: Create a testable hypothesis that outlines the expected outcome of your bet. This should be specific, measurable and aligned with your business and product strategy.
- There are several formats you can use for documenting your key hypothesis. The simplest and my preference is to write it out in this way:
- We believe that [doing this]
- for [these people]
- will achieve [this outcome]
- We'll know this is true when we see [this market feedback].

- **Choose a testing method:** Select the most appropriate testing method for your hypothesis. This could be A/B testing, user research, or a combination of methods. There might be multiple methods to test but focus on the method that gives you the fastest time to value. The faster you learn, the more iterations you can do."
- **Implement and execute:** Put your testing plan into action and gather data. Be sure to clearly define how you will measure success and what data points you will track.
- **Analyse and interpret data:** Review the data you have collected, and analyse the results. Use this data to validate or invalidate your hypothesis and make informed decisions about the direction of your product strategy.
- **Iterate and improve:** Based on the results of your testing, iterate and improve your product strategy. Use the insights gained from testing to make changes and improve the product.

It's important to note that testing and experimentation are an ongoing process. Product strategies should be regularly re-visited and updated based on new data and insights. By using this structured approach, product leaders can de-risk their opportunities and make data-driven decisions about the direction of their products.

We could easily write a book on testing and experimentation, and there are lots out there that dig into this subject. We recommend Testing Business Ideas from Strategyzer as a starting point.

To organise your strategy, it's a good idea to not have all your strategies be high risk. Review the section on "You Already Have a Strategy" to identify what is working and what is not. The organisation's risk appetite and team size will dictate the spread of risk across strategies. A starting point is 60% low risk, 30% medium risk, and 10% high risk which are basic tolerances used for good portfolio management across many use industries. You can adjust these based on your particular preferences.

In conclusion, testing and experimentation play a crucial role in a successful product strategy. By creating hypotheses, testing assumptions and generating data, product teams can make informed decisions and adjust their strategy accordingly. This can lead to a more efficient use of time and resources and a better performing product. To get started, it is important to consider how you will test your strategies and to organise them in a way that aligns with your organisation's risk appetite.

7

Empower Teams

A good product strategy is essential for empowering teams to develop software products effectively. It provides a clear vision and direction for the product, and helps teams understand how their work fits into the larger goals of the company.

Here are a few ways in which a good product strategy can empower teams:

- **Defines clear goals and priorities**: A well-defined product strategy helps teams understand what the product is trying to achieve, and what the most important features and goals are. This helps teams prioritise their work and focus on the things that will have the greatest impact.
- **Provides a shared understanding**: A good product strategy helps teams understand the context and reasoning behind the product, as well as how it fits into the larger market and industry. This shared understanding helps teams work together more effectively, as they all have a clear

understanding of the product's purpose and direction.

- **Facilitates decision-making:** A good product strategy provides a framework for making decisions about the product, including what features to build, what technologies to use, and how to allocate resources. This helps teams make informed decisions that align with the overall goals of the product.
- **Enables flexibility and adaptability:** A good product strategy should be flexible and adaptable, allowing teams to pivot and adjust as the market and customer needs change. This helps teams stay agile and respond to new opportunities and challenges.

It is generally considered best practice for software teams to be empowered to identify and solve problems on their own, rather than being dictated solutions from higher levels of the organisation. This allows teams to have a greater sense of ownership over their work and can lead to more innovative and effective solutions.

There are several ways that teams can be empowered to engage in problem-solving and opportunity identification:

Encourage a culture of continuous learning: Encourage team members to continuously learn about new technologies, methodologies, and best practices in their field. This will help them stay up to date with the latest developments and be better equipped to identify and solve problems.

Foster a culture of transparency and open communication:

Encourage team members to speak up and share their thoughts and ideas openly. This can help to identify problems and opportunities earlier and allow for more effective collaboration.

Emphasise ownership and accountability: Encourage team members to take ownership of their work and be accountable for the outcomes. This can help to build a sense of responsibility and commitment to delivering quality work.

By empowering software teams to identify and solve problems on their own, organisations can create a more dynamic and innovative culture that is better equipped to navigate the constantly changing landscape of software development.

8

Build Confidence

A common issue found in our research is that although many organization has the right functions, they are isolated. This makes it difficult for teams or leaders to draw a straight line between them. By doing so they can make more autonomous decisions to align back to the direction of the business in their everyday decisions with less oversight.

Business strategy might happen, but it is done only with the board and executives and never shared with the rationale of what this means for the team's day to day. As a Product Leader, it is your job to bring that context together as it pertains to product investments.

If you are going to take on this important role of aligning and communicating the product direction, then it is important to keep your target audience in mind. This could be an engineer, executive or board member, so you need to communicate in a language that is accessible to them all.

Some of the best ways we have found to build shared understanding include:

- **Use a structure that guides the reader from wherever they are in the organisation into the space you want them to be thinking.** This is often the first place the most non-product people get lost when reading documents that get straight into the detail without addressing where this sits within the business and how it relates to the reader's context. Fortunately, this book provides you with a structure that will help you land the reader from the business level, all the way down through to the current focus of product teams.
- **Write as plainly as possible without too much jargon.** Remove any references to frameworks or technical terms or, if you can't, link to a simple explanation so your audience can still continue to use your document. Eschewing technical terms may feel you are "dumbing it down" but is actually the opposite, as if you can't describe things in simple and accessible terms it shows you may not truly understand them yourself. This can be a hard skill to master after many years of working so deeply in the product field, but it is invaluable in the alignment it brings within your organisation.
- **Use or link to sources as much as possible to show you are not building in isolation.** We expand on this later in the book, but when filling out your strategy, it is important to show that you understand and are interested in the other work going on around the business. By the simple act of linking to other sources e.g. a competitive analysis, it shows that you are looking and listening to what others are doing and you are interested in working together. Just like any

good article or scientific paper, linking to your sources also gives confidence that whatever position you take, your document is built upon the work of others and has a solid foundation.

We must highlight that this focus on building shared under-standing is one of the most important aspects of developing any strategy and without it, your strategy is likely to never be used in practice. Take the time to refine your strategy to make it as essential and easy to use as possible, as it has the leverage to speak for you and guide the team when you aren't there.

IV

Discovery

9

You Already Have a Strategy

Congratulations on having made it this far. You should now have enough of a perspective on why it is worth writing this strategy and the way you and your team can start approaching it from a new perspective. This will lead to a more connected and confident understanding of where you are investing your time and energy.

Before we get to the building where we want to go, though, it is a good idea to briefly understand where we are and how we got here. Therefore, we recommend a discovery period where you gather as much of the existing material across the business and use it to inform, guide and benchmark how you proceed.

Whether you have a written strategy document or not, strategy is a set of choices that have been made to move in a direction. It is useful to understand what choices have been made so far and use that momentum to navigate the way you show up in the market vs the way you actually do.

Step 1 - Gather all your vision and mission documents.

This could be on your intranet, in slides to the board or even your website. The executive team often writes them to the organisation or your marketing and sales teams to customers. These are often many statements about why your company exists and how you help the customer in the market.

Gather as many of these as possible, put them in the one place and see how well they match. Do they match or diverge in any way? Note that down for your conversations later. If they don't exist then that is ok too. Make it explicit though that these things are missing and would help if they existed. You can make the call with your team whether it would be more valuable to develop them now or come back to this later.

Step 2 - Write down all the features your product currently has in market

Take all of the features you currently have in the market and put them down on a page. When we are working in more of an output-based approach, sometimes we neglect to understand the overall theme or customer outcome we are trying to serve.

Take all your features and try to group them into themes. You will need to take things up a level and try to think of the outcome that the feature is trying to serve. Is it helping your customer collaborate, for example? You could also think about this as the job to be done when trying to group them.

Once grouped, you will see the strategies that you have been using this far within the market. Typically, we see two patterns emerge from this.

1. You will see two or three strategies where most of your features show up. This is the value your product supports in the market. It is interesting to see if the decisions made for your product match the vision, marketing and sales materials - are your product teams delivering on what is being promised within the business and to the market?.

2. The other pattern you may see is one feature in each strategy. When you see this, it can be a sign that you are trying too many things with not enough focus to cut through in any area. Your product may try to be all things to all people rather than focussing on a particular customer and their needs.

41

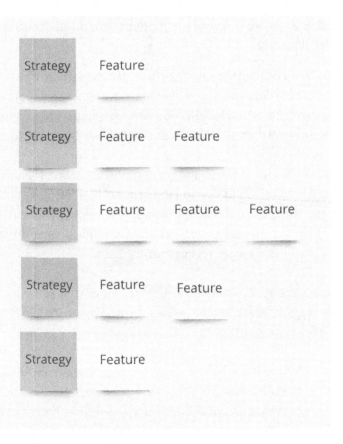

*Align all your features to themes or outcomes
and see where your main clusters form.*

Actions

· Gather all your vision and mission documents.
· Write down all the features your product currently has in market

YOU ALREADY HAVE A STRATEGY

10

Talk to Customers

Your business and product do not exist inside the walls of your business. They exist with your customers and users, where they choose to use your product and engage with your business, in the way they want to.

In the previous sections we have talked about what you need to do to understand your business strategy and how your product is appearing in the market even if it is not explicitly written down. And we have introduced the mindsets and activities that are required to develop, socialise and deliver on your product strategy.

As a product leader, having scheduled time with your customers is incredibly important. Outside of your strategy work, having a deep understanding based on first hand conversations creates context in a way you cannot get only from synthesised conversations and research done by others. If you do not already have this as a ritual as part of your routine, take it on.

Take a moment to reflect on the findings from the previous section where we outline how to identify the strategy you already have. Consider that these strategy groupings now need to be validated and extended upon. This is where talking to customers comes into play to extend your confidence in these groupings, where they are adding value, where they are performing and underperforming. Holding conversations with your customers will help you build out your product strategy based on what you learn from these conversations.

When having these conversations make sure to speak to different tiers of customers and users. Understanding where each customer/user is experiencing value vs where they are not, will build context you can use later in the development of your strategy.

Some example questions you could use are:

- How would you feel if you could no longer use (insert your product name here)?
- A) Very disappointed B) Somewhat disappointed C) Not disappointed
- What type of people do you think would most benefit from our product?
- What is the main benefit you receive from using our product?
- How could we improve our product for you?
- After each of these questions make sure to ask why they answered the way they did, this will lead to further context.

Once you have interviewed these users, take the time to synthesise your research. Once synthesised, look at how the learnings align or don't align to the groupings you have identified out of the previous section, or from your current product strategy.

This is also the time to look at your product usage data, experiment findings and business data to see how this aligns to your groupings. If you have not done so, now is the time. If you have done so, include that as part of collating the information from the previous sections with your customer research.

Actions

1. Summary of what customers see as value
2. Synthesise to understand where value is created in your product
3. Align on how your product is supporting your business goals (or not)

11

Use Data

Inadequate or ineffective measurement can lead to problems for product leaders in prioritising work, communicating value, and building trust within their teams, peers, and organisation. Without understanding how work impacts the business and users, product teams may struggle to prioritise and celebrate their work, leading to low morale and churn. At senior and executive levels, the lack of measurement leads to difficulty in reporting, communicating progress, and making informed decisions. This can result in disempowerment, inefficiency, stress, and loss of trust in the product team. To develop effective measurement skills, we recommend checking out Corinna Stukan's "The Insights Driven Product Manager".

As a product leader, data in various forms will underpin your decision making. In this section we will bring together, summarise and connect the different data sources we discuss throughout the initial sections of this book.

Let's first look at data that you have collected on your existing product and features. This data is sourced from your product analytics, support feedback, win/loss analysis, customer interviews etc. In the section You Already Have a Product Strategy, you pulled together the features and functionality you already have in the market, you have looked at the usage and effectiveness of these features and you have grouped these into themes to provide you with where your product strategy is in its current state.

In this synthesis you are able to identify gaps in your current offering, opportunities to optimise and even see where there are gaps in functionality which will improve your product. This data provides you with the foundation to work from in developing your product strategy.

By building out this foundation, you can then pull in the data from talking to customers, current in-flight experiments and tests as well as anecdotal evidence from other teams, like your sales or customer success teams who regularly speak with customers. The synthesis of this will help you see if the work in progress matches what your data is telling you.

As an example you might find that there is 60% of work that is miss aligned to where you are seeing opportunity based on the data you have. This is an indicator to dig into why this work is taking place, and ask the question, should it be done at all?

Once you have brought together the "what's so" in the data. Have a clear picture of what is working and what is not. It is time to start to define your product strategy. Leveraging the data you have brought together to help inform the strategy and support your narrative.

Actions

Collect as many of the following data sets as you can. Here are some examples (non exhaustive) of types of data you should be leveraging:

1. Product behaviour analytics from tools like Mixpanel or Amplitude
2. Customer data such as Customer Acquisition Cost (CAC) and Lifetime Value (LTV) as well a Customer Satisfaction (CSAT)
3. Synthesised insights from customer interviews.
4. Qual and quant data from customer research, surveys and experiments
5. Sales and marketing data, channel performance, value proposition and messaging success data
6. Customer support data
7. Financial data such as revenue projections, sales targets, human resource budgets, targets set for product
8. Market data such as competitive analysis and industry trends.

V

The Framework

12

The Players

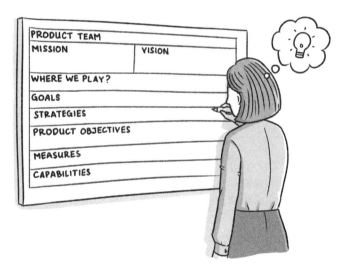

Your first draft of this strategy may be built in isolation with information you have on hand, but eventually you will need to involve some key players in your organisation that make important trade offs and choices with varying levels of granularity.

The three major areas and layers of this effort are:

Executives

Is anyone in the C-level of your business who works with your CEO to effectively "run the business". They represent the investors, board and will define why the business exists. They have a responsibility to their stakeholders and so must define their expectations and validate the return on investment that your team and product will generate. The two major parts they contribute to your strategy are:

- The Vision - Why does this business exist? Why was it set up?
- Goals - What financial and other performance metrics must the business hit to satisfy its duty to its investors?

Product leaders

Could be the CPO, VP, Head of or Directors of Product, Anyone who manages multiple teams and streams of product development. They are accountable for contributing to the goals outlined above but also need to give the teams valuable constraints so they can develop enough of a product market fit to be a compelling offer in the market. Areas they need to detail are:

- The Playing Field - What markets and customers must we prioritise?
- Product Strategies - How will we compete and win in those

spaces, considering our competencies, competition and opportunities?
- Measures - How will we measure responsible and continued investment so we know when to shift strategies?
- Capabilities - What will we need to execute against this plan and succeed?

Product Teams

Are your cross-functional product teams aligned with the Strategy and Vision to drive a consistent and compounded customer experience? If they don't, you will end up with a bunch of singularly valuable features or products, but a customer experience that is confusing to navigate. The Product Teams handle:

- Opportunities - Are bodies of work that the customers find desirable but also are viable to satisfy the business goals and feasible from a capability point of view.

In the following sections, we will go in depth with each of these areas, provide examples of how we have approached it as well as helpful frameworks if you need to undertake building these yourself.

13

Vision

The highest level common reference point across your entire organisation is usually your company vision. A vision statement outlines why your company exists. What purpose does it serve? Some people can get caught up thinking that the purpose of all businesses is to make money. That can be the case, but is often not the sole reason. If that were true, then why is your company not selling other products? Why did your founder/s start the company? There may be a lot more lucrative ways to make money. There is a group of customers that the company serves so what are their needs and what does that need look like in decades to come?

Depending on your organisation, the words "mission" and "vision" may be used interchangeably. It doesn't matter what it's called, it still needs to answer "Why do you exist?"

A vision is also likely never to be achieved, as often it is an aspirational perfect state your organisation will strive for. We can never deem it "Done" but will always seek to improve the current state.

A company vision is also not a strategy, and it is not a goal. A strategy is the decisions the company has made on how they are going to aim to achieve the company vision, and a goal is a shorter term milestone to fulfil a strategy. Both can be achieved and will often be revised frequently. Visions are only revised when there are massive shifts in the market, technologies or customers in that space.

Some examples of company visions are:

Strava

> Strava is Swedish for "strive," which epitomizes our attitude and ambition: We're a passionate and committed team, unified by our mission to build the most engaged community of athletes in the world.

Microsoft

> To empower every person and every organisation on the planet to achieve more.

Netflix

> To entertain the world

Actions

> 1. Go through your website, annual report or any other

company document and find your company vision.

2. If you don't have one then have a chat with your CEO about establishing one as a unifying force to give your people and processes a sense of purpose.

3. Ask yourself and people in the company;

4. Why does the company exist?

5. Who does it serve?

6. What are their needs?

7. How can this help the world?

8. Create a strategy canvas on a whiteboard so you can construct and share these parts as you find them.

14

Goals

Now that we have a good understanding of why the business exists, we need to understand what we expect of it in the short and medium term. This is where business goals come into play. We are chunking down and getting more specific, slowly adding constraints so we can focus teams on what is most important now.

From our research, we have heard stories of Product Leaders who are asked to come up with business goals. While this can be a wonderful opportunity to be a part of the process, it is ultimately not a product but an executive responsibility. Businesses, and especially executive teams, have a responsibility to the board and investors and so business goals should be aligned with those expectations.

Often these goals will be financial as that's what ultimately all your efforts boil down to and product teams are usually shielded from this complexity rather than empowering them to see the entire picture.

We encourage you to find these goals and make them a part of your strategy as it shows your interest and focus on helping to achieve them. You will often find them in your board report, other executive documents or just ask your CEO for them.

If you receive over four or five goals, then this is a warning sign that the business is not focussed around what really matters and what will move the business forward in the next few quarters. It is best to address this with your executive team first, as just as clear focus can create optimal outcomes, too many competing focuses can create confusion, and that is something you don't want to spread in your teams.

Here are some examples of what a company goal my look like

- Sales - Hit $100 M in sales using existing channels
- Revenue Per Order - Increase average deal size by 25% with upsells
- Churn Rate - Reduce churn to <5% through improved customer support

We have seen organisations where there were 15-20 goals and often teams just remember the top three or four and the rest are forgotten.

The value of your product leadership is in taking these business goals and making them relevant to your product team and helping them understand how they translate into product decisions. If your topline goal is to increase sales by 20%, you need to help teams decide between feature A or B. Feature A is really cool and many customers are asking for but Feature B is something that has shown up a lot in your lost deals. In this case, you would need to help teams understand that the priority needs to be to unlock revenue from new customers. We will go into more detail.

Actions

- Find your company goals and add them to your whiteboard
- Discuss with your CEO if there are over four and ask which would be the most important to focus on

15

The Playing Field

This may be the most important part of this book. The Playing Field is the section of the framework which supports product leaders in making decisions on what markets and customers to focus on, and which not to.

It is where we define the market which will allow us to focus our efforts where it matters most. The playing field is the space that sets the boundaries of the work the business will undertake, and provides guidance on the players in the market; competitors and customers.

The Playing Field is the connector between business goals and product strategy. It should be co-owned by the executive team. Spending time to get this section complete, socialised and aligned with executives and leaders is a key action product leaders need to take in order for their strategy to be effective.

Depending on the type of organisation you work in the work may have already been done. If it hasn't or is unclear, take the time to interview the executives in the team. To get their views, documents and experience with what market the business is in, who the customers are and who the competitors are.

This interview process can take many shapes, and there are so many tools to understand a market, we use.... And I trust you will use your skills to select your method. What we really want as an outcome is clarity and alignment on:

- What is the market the business is in?
- What are the businesses that make up the market?
- Who are the competitors in the market?
- What is your business position in the market?
- What is the size of the market?
- What is the Total Addressable Market (TAM)?
- What is the portion of the market (TAM) you can capture based on your business mode or Serviceable Addressable Market (SAM)?
- What is the percentage of the SAM you can realistically capture or Serviceable Obtainable Market (SOM)?
- What adjacencies are there to the market?
- What are the customer profiles within the market?
- Who are the personas that cut across the market?
- What are the forces at play within the market?

If you feel like these questions are outside of your current skill set it can be valuable to have an analyst or product marketing manager help you with these questions.

Actions

- When it comes to summarising the outcomes of your inter-views and research, start with playing back what you have learned to the people you have interviewed, then go wider and deeper.
- Ask them what's missing, what could be clearer. This process helps you build trust and relationships across the business. Facilitates conversations and finds common language that can be reused, and shapes the picture in a way you can have a shared understanding.

16

Strategies

One motivation for writing this book was from seeing organisations where the Product Strategy was a monolithic slide that
was talked about once and never really referred to ever again. By
doing this, the leaders had turned strategy into a one way take
it or leave it dynamic where you either agreed with the strategy
or didn't. It either worked or didn't. We knew that this wasn't
the way it worked when the strategy interacted with customers,
the market, and competitors. Some things worked, and some
didn't. Some things should continue to be invested in and others
were better left as they were to make the most of the limited
resources every company has.

It was also clear that many organisations had a hard time letting
go of failed experiments or pivoting when something wasn't
working. Part of this is the mindset that we wrote about earlier
where the strategy is put forward as a bold proclamation that
must work as it's what we said we would do. Instead, by breaking
the strategy apart into a set of strategies, we turn them into a set
of experiments that will survive based on data. No one knows

if they will work or not and we let the market decide if they are worth continuing to invest in.

Strategies describe how you are going to win in the market that you have chosen and are heavily influenced by the competitors, the market you have chosen, and the vision that you have for your business. Some strategies you may need to have because that is what the market expects as table stakes, while others you may focus on because it differentiates you and pushes you further towards your vision.

Strategies are also outcome focussed on what they do for the customer. For example, you might compete in collaboration by providing chat, mentions or workboard in your app. You might compete in risk management by highlighting issues to your customers so they can take action. Your decision to invest in these spaces should be based upon whether they delight your customers, improve your business, and differentiate you from your competitors.

Gibson Biddle, Former Netflix/Chegg VP Product developed a model for this that he calls DHM. He suggests your strategies should

- Delight customers in;
- Margin enhancing and;
- Hard to copy ways;

Let's break these down a little more

- Delighting customers means you are building things that

customers find useful and help them achieve an outcome.

- Margin enhancing means that this is related to contributing to the goal outlined already. Do they reduce churn or unlock revenue?
- Hard to copy means they are worth investing in because they will differentiate you from your competitors and can't be easily replicated, removing any advantage you have when competitors do the same.

We should note that not everything can be hard to copy. Some strategies may be minimum requirements for your industry. Customers will get very dissatisfied if something is not there but that offering or feature doesn't provide differentiation for your company. It is important to have a mix of strategies as it's unlikely that everything you do will be hard to copy.

Once you have these strategies, it is important to understand that this has come up with the best information you have. What you really have is a set of hypotheses that you will use lean approaches to build, measure, learn and continue to invest into the strategy. If from your tests and data there isn't value in continuing to invest, it will be important to prioritise or remove that strategy so your resources can be allocated the most effectively.

Actions

- Take all your current features and sort them into groups using a card sorting method.
- Do this a few times with a few people, even customers to see if you get differing results.

- Name these groups but the theme or outcome that it produces for the customer e.g. Personalisation, Collaboration or Automation.
- Share with your team that these are the ways you are competing in the market and see if it matches how they and customers are communicating.
- Start to think about how you can measure the effectiveness of each strategy and if it is getting you towards your goal. Is there another strategy that makes more sense to invest in?

17

Measures

Measures are how you will keep track of how your strategies, and the opportunities you are executing on are performing.

There are two areas you are going to be measuring when using the Product Strategy Bridge. The first is how effective your strategies are in guiding work to hit the business goal the strategy supports. The second is the measurement of the opportunities that support the strategies.

Your product strategies should have a direct connection to the business goals the product team is responsible for. If you have strategies that are not connected to these goals you should remove them, as that work will be hard if not impossible to justify and is not aligned to the business.

If you have strategies you believe need to be pursued that do not align, then you must work with your executives to either create a new goal or make changes to existing goals to support your strategy. The key here is to get alignment with your executives.

Initially your measures for the identified opportunities may not have a foundation to support them, as an example you may have to make a hypothesis on what the outcome will be from an experiment or test that is part of your opportunities.

The goal here is for you to manage the strategies and the business goals they relate to. Your team should be empowered to identify, validate and then build or execute on the opportunities they have identified which align to the strategies you have defined. This is the work of making your bridging strategy testable, and the most important part of this work.

Early on in implementing your testable bridging strategy you will need to work closely with your teams to set out and break down the opportunities which align to the strategies you have defined. Setting up a regular check in with your teams to review progress on the measures of success that have been agreed on for each of the opportunities is critical.

Once you have settled into a comfortable rhythm and the teams are owning the work, you can reduce the frequency. I would suggest that monthly is a good target to get to. And it will depend on the rhythm of the team's ability to execute. In a smaller startup that ships daily or weekly, fortnightly might be the way to go to start with.

You may have several strategies that sit under one goal, be clear on what metrics each strategy will move in relation to the goal.

- You may have several opportunities that align to a strategy, we have found it to be good practice to not have opportunities align to several strategies. Keep the opportunities themed to a strategy, at least to start with.

- Each opportunity needs to have a hypothesis and measures for pass/fail. We have found this practice of converting all opportunities to a hypothesis supports the teams in their work when evaluating which opportunities should be prioritised and how they will measure the success of the opportunity.

Actions

- Align strategies to goals
- Work with product teams to identify opportunities that underpin the strategies you have set
- Empower your product teams to de-risk the opportunities through testing and experimentation

18

Opportunities

The definition of opportunity is; a time or set of circumstances that makes it possible to do something. Within the context of the bridging strategy opportunities are bounded work packages which should deliver value for your customer and/or your business and should ladder up to one of the strategies in the framework.

That's pretty dense so let's unpack it by answering these questions:

1. How do we define the work packages?
2. How do we know that these work packages will deliver value?
3. How do we align these work packages to our strategies and goals?

How do we define the work packages?

When we started creating this framework we were being asked to pull together a product strategy based on what was currently possible based on the existing technical capabilities for the organisation we worked for. We found this limiting, constraining and with a focus drawing from the past, not opportunity for the future.. We are not saying it's wrong, just that working with what you have already, recombining the current focus and capabilities will only get you so far.

So we decided to take two steps, the first being to define and break out what technical capabilities existed, see the section on Technical Capabilities for a deeper dive. And the second to include opportunities to increase the scope so the team or teams working on the strategy had a space to identify and validate new ways of creating value.

It is no mistake that this section is called opportunities, more on that shortly but let's consider bets, initiatives or features, common language in product teams. And depending on your organisation you may use some or all of these descriptors to give more context to opportunities.

The key is to do so in a standardised way. A bet is just that it has intrinsic risk and although it could yield a result it equally could not. An initiative is a bounded piece of work to accomplish a goal or solve a specific problem for your organisation or for your user or customer, an initiative therefore has a direction and can be measured if it has had some validation against it. And finally a feature should be well defined and thus should already be de-risked, its value understood before it is built.

You can see there is a theme to these definitions which is that each name represents a level of risk, and depending on the appetite of your business and/or strategy for innovation and risk you can take on more or less of each type as you progress.

What we recognised early on is that there is no structure to link these different definitions together under the banner of opportunities.

The list looks like this:

Opportunities

- Bet - high risk if this is shipped without de-risking
- Initiative - medium risk if shipped, may require breaking down as its validated
- Feature - low risk if shipped as it has moved through validation

They key here is that all opportunities should have a key hypothesis that sits behind the work, that drives the rigour of testing and learning. There are many product books on hypothesis driven product development. From my perspective the "why" here is that a hypothesis driven approach to your product strategy drives common language, reduces bias, makes your work measurable and therefore reduces risk and allows you and your teams to capture the learnings in a way that can be documented and shared with stakeholders and referenced as required.

How do we know that these work packages will deliver value?

By introducing key hypotheses as the scaffolding of the opportunities that sit underneath your strategies you give your teams the tools to de-risk their work. On the flip side you gain confidence that the work being done will deliver the expected value set out in the hypothesis.

The hypothesis-driven approach lends itself to being measured, not just the obviously measurable outcome of the experiments or tests we have defined to de-risk the hypothesis but we can count the number of hypotheses we are testing, the cost of them and the time taken to validate these.

We can start measuring our experiment velocity, e.g. "we're running 3x $1,000 experiments per week". We can also measure our speed to learning, this is how we quantify the value of the lessons we are learning from failed and successful experiments.

Measurability is the value that is unlocked by the hypothesis-driven approach and makes it easy for us as product leaders to understand how to de-risk, plan, budget for and undertake the execution of our testable strategy.

How do we align these work packages to our strategies and goals?

As your strategies have been set prior, provide these to your team ahead of the workshop giving them time to define their key hypothesis for their work. Give them the template ahead of time and have them align their hypothesis to the strategies. So once you get to the workshop, the interactions and conversations are around if the opportunities are bucketed under the correct strategy. This workshop will also allow you and your team to align the strategies to the capabilities and measures in the framework.

Actions

- Define and standardise the language used for "work packages" within your organisation.
- Align work packages to the organisation's strategy and goals.
- Develop a hypothesis-driven approach, focusing on reducing bias, increasing measurability, and capturing learnings.
- Use a hypothesis-driven approach to de-risk opportunities and gain confidence in the value that will be delivered by the work packages.
- Break down opportunities as they are validated and move towards a low-risk state.
- Measure the number of hypotheses being tested, the cost, and the time taken to validate them.
- Document and share the learnings with stakeholders, and use them to guide future product strategy.
- Be proactive in identifying new ways of creating value for

the customer and business.

19

Capabilities - People

Depending on how ambitious your strategy is you will need to consider whether you have the right people on board to deliver. This often happens when you are innovating and improving your strategy into new domains you haven't operated in before or you have an aggressive timeline in which to achieve your strategy.

There could be many ways your strategy describes where you are going to play and how you are going to win, which can require additional skills and experience to help. For example, if you are expanding into new markets or geographies, it pays to have someone on the team who has had experience with your product in those markets. Not doing so can have you overlooked and can create failures from simple details that could easily have been avoided.

Another way you might need to consider people is by their skill set. For example, data science is becoming more and more of an opportunity for companies to leverage customer data to enhance products with personalisation. To do this successfully though requires people with a sound understanding of the different ways of creating data products.

This idea of skills gaps extends to every team, though. Need to create a better understanding of how your products and services fit together? Maybe you need a service designer. Need to redesign your site and improve your branding? Maybe you need a front-end engineer with design systems experience.

Without getting into too much detail you just need to recognise these skills and be ready to have a conversation with your leadership about how you might fill these gaps. You might consider upskilling the people on your current team or need to start recruitment of a new team member to get them onboard in time. Have these options ready so when you discuss your strategy with your stakeholders you can balance the challenge of acquiring these capabilities against the value of the strategy you are considering.

Actions

- Assess the skills and experience of your current team to identify any gaps that may hinder the successful implementation of your strategy.
- Consider the specific skills and experience required for new markets or geographies that your strategy may expand into.
- Evaluate the need for specialised skills such as data science, service design, and frontend engineering to support the execution of your strategy.
- Have a conversation with your leadership about how to fill any identified skills gaps, including options for upskilling

current team members or recruiting new team members.
- Balance the challenge of acquiring necessary capabilities against the potential value of the strategy under consideration.
- Plan for recruitment and training/upskilling of team members to ensure they are onboard in time for the execution of the strategy.

20

Capabilities - Technology

Depending on the size of your organisation and the complexity of your product, as a product leader you may need to guide your teams in this section.

This section should be workshopped by the product teams when they are aligning their opportunities, setting measures for success for each of the opportunities and aligning this to the technical capabilities that already exist, are on the roadmap or need to be proposed as part of the overall product strategy.

The value of this work cannot be overstated. This section is where each product team can identify where on their roadmap, if at all an opportunity will sit. It provides an invaluable reference for prioritisation and underpins feasibility which in turn can be used to prioritise work.

Referencing the Opportunities section of the framework take each of the key hypothesis, initiative or feature and identify what technical capabilities already exist that can be leveraged or recombined to deliver the opportunity. Where capabilities are missing or work is required to leverage it this provides the guidance to effort to implement. Where technical capabilities are not present, this becomes a conversation on when, if at all, it could be built and more importantly is the value to the business or the user or customer enough to have this prioritised. And if prioritised what work is affected.

As a product leader you will be working with your CTO or equivalent to map this out, support your teams in prioritising and where not enough data is present to make trade off calls supporting them in executing research, tests or experiments to get the validation required so that the prioritisation calls can be made.

As a product leader having a clear picture of the effort will allow you to build out a cost model based on all your teams mapping of current work in flight, the initiatives and key hypotheses they have identified based on the strategies you have provided them as guidance.

This work will capture the goals your teams want to achieve with your technology. Working with your CTO breaks down their work into functional requirements, look for commonalities and then map to existing and upcoming capabilities. This work will feed into your cost model.

In conclusion, it is essential for a product leader to have a clear understanding of the technical capabilities required to deliver their product strategy. By workshopping with their teams, identifying opportunities and aligning them with existing or proposed technical capabilities, product leaders can make informed decisions on prioritisation and feasibility. This, in turn, supports the overall cost model and allows for effective planning and execution of the product strategy. By working closely with their CTO or equivalent, product leaders can ensure that their teams have the necessary skills and resources to deliver on the desired outcome. Overall, this section of the framework is crucial for a successful product strategy, and as a product leader, it is essential to effectively guide and manage this process.

Actions

- Hold a workshop with product teams to align opportunities and set measures for success for each opportunity.
- Reference the Opportunities section of the framework and take each of the key hypothesis, initiative or feature and identify what technical capabilities already exist that can be leveraged or recombined to deliver the opportunity.
- Identify where technical capabilities are missing or work is required to leverage it and use this information to guide effort to implement.
- Where technical capabilities are not present, engage in a conversation about when and if it could be built and more importantly, the value to the business or the user or customer to have it prioritised.
- Work with CTO or equivalent to map out the technical capabilities and support teams in prioritising and executing research, tests or experiments to get the validation required to make trade-off calls.
- Build a cost model based on all teams' mapping of current work in flight, the initiatives and key hypotheses they have

identified based on the strategies provided as guidance.
- Break down the work into functional requirements, look for commonalities and map to existing and upcoming capabilities to feed into the cost model.
- Continuously review and socialise the work with peers and stakeholders to ensure alignment with product strategies and business goals.
- Effectively guide and manage this process as a product leader to ensure a successful product strategy.

VI

Write it down, and share it

21

Product Leaders

As a product leader, it is your responsibility to coordinate, socialise, align, and document your product strategy. This does not mean you do all the work; being effective in this work means managing to completion the components of the bridging strategy.

Once you have the outcomes generated in Discovery, Talk to Customers, and Use Data, it is time to pull together what you have learned. This section is about that process and will guide you through the steps.

Write it down

There are many formats you can leverage to bring your content together. Narrative writing is one that we have an affinity for. It allows for logical groupings of the opportunities (or problems) you are looking to work on through your strategy, so that you can communicate it back easily.

Start with a summary of what you have uncovered in your research with your executive teams, through talking to customers, and data. This should paint a clear picture of where there are problems and opportunities.

The key is to keep asking yourself "so what"; "so what if we solve this problem, or validate the opportunity?" This will guide you to linking the different pockets of information you have collected. This will provide you with the logical groupings, which you can then use to speculate on what strategy or strategies you will need to use to guide your business towards its vision.

Once you have written up your first version of the narrative, take it to some of your peers you spoke with early on. Get them to read it and request that they challenge you on your groupings, logic, and linking of data. Rework as you see fit based on the feedback you receive. Do this several times until you have alignment on the groupings, language, and data.

Share it

The next place to take your newly formed narrative is to your product managers, share it with them ahead of a meeting. In the meeting, take the time to listen to how they see what you have written, listen for discrepancies, and be curious. Ask why they see it that way, what insights do they have that you may have missed? Incorporate feedback where relevant.

Be aware that your product managers may not have all the context you have; is this an opportunity to share that with them? Yes! And where they have data to back a different view, take the time to incorporate this. Ask, how will this help you with your work?

Next, it's time to socialise with your peers again, use the same process as with your product managers. Make sure to listen for the language they are using to describe and playback what they are reading in your narrative. Ask your peers how they would use this work. What is the best format for them to keep it in existence and useful?

You may need to make adjustments to format and groupings based on the socialisation, to be clear this is not an exercise in mediocrity or pleasing, make sure to uncover the why behind the changes and reference the data.

22

Product Managers

Once the narrative and strategies have been developed and re-fined through collaboration, it is important to empower product managers to own and implement them within their teams. This can be achieved through a workshop with the product managers, where opportunities that align with the strategies are identified and current work is evaluated for alignment. Any work that is not aligned should be re-evaluated and potentially removed to make room for new, aligned opportunities.

To guide their strategic planning, product managers should conduct research to deepen their understanding of where to invest time and effort. They should use the data collected and shared by the product leader to align their work with the business goals and provide strategies for decision making. This research should be used to identify any untapped opportunities.

The next step is to turn the data and research into well-formed hypotheses, initiatives and features. Product managers should share their work with their teams and gather feedback, making any necessary adjustments and conducting further research as needed. They should then present their plan to their product leader, communicating their goals for the upcoming month, quarter, and year and using data to support their hypotheses and strategies. Finally, the product managers should share their work with their peers and socialise the strategies, highlighting how they align with the product strategy, playing field, and business goals.

23

Strategy Example

Product Strategy

This document seeks to provide a summary of the market opportunity and the direction that we will take over the next few years to align leaders and stakeholders

An example of how a strategy page might be written.

24

Use Our Template

Product Team	
Mission	Vision

Playing Field

Goals

Strategies

Product Objectives (tactics)

Measures

Capabilities

You can also access templates on our Miro board.

VII

Conclusion

25

Start Now

Congratulations on having made it this far. It is a significant investment in yourself, your organisation and your team to have started down this road. But it doesn't stop there. If this is your first time reading through our playbook, then as we have talked about throughout the book, try to get started immediately on a whiteboard, wiki page or slide deck to gather all the pieces that you are already aware of that fit into the areas we have outlined. In short, get started as the momentum you have now is valuable and important to getting to your first draft of your product strategy.

Once you have gathered everything that comes to mind, put in sixty minutes in the next few days to refine and gather more pieces. You want to race as fast as you can to your first draft so you can start the sharing process with your direct team and expand that influence around the business. Remember to always ask for more information from your peers to tap into the work and thinking that has already been produced, but it is your decision on whether or not it is relevant.

Do it Again

Once you have your first strategy, share it with anyone who will listen and repeat it at any chance you can get, then you will need to update it on a regular cadence. Typically, this will be each quarter where you will go through many of the same steps with the same artefacts but with the lens of "What has changed?".

Have your priorities changed based on new information? Is a strategy not looking as valuable as you first thought? Is a strategy proving more valuable. Look at this update as a reallocation of your investment performance. The investment of your team's time. Some areas will perform well and you need to consider upping your investment and others will be underperforming. Here, you need to be not too quick to pull resources away from a strategy. A strategy needs a quarter or two to find its feet, so don't be too quick in relocating your team's time so you can see a strategy flourish. Once a strategy is not working, then share with your team your intention to change direction so it does not surprise them when this does not continue.

26

Acknowledgments

We want to thank all those who contributed and guided us during the writing of this book. Your encouragement and feedback was greatly appreciated and shows how supportive the product community can be.

Special thanks to everyone who talked with us about their experiences and helped us edit this book. We couldn't have done it without you.

- Mike Burke
- Lenka Chadaj
- Jerllin Cheng
- Jack Chivers
- Sebastien Eckersley-Maslin
- Cheryl Gledhill
- Thommy Jerneskog
- Mandar Karlekar
- Lily Kingston

- Michael Lansdowne
- Amir Marzouk
- Angus Mcdonald
- Ben Reid
- Jonny Schneider
- Jasper Streit
- Corinna Stukan
- David Wang
- Benjamin Wirtz

About the Author

Working with the Honey Insurance team as Principal Product Manager, Novel Channel Partners, Alejandro Patterson is responsible for validating and building experiences and integrations that turn insurance upside down! Passionate about improving startup success, he mentors at Founders Institute and speaks regularly on validation, prototyping and experimentation.

As a Director of Product, Simon Hilton is responsible for leading and growing product teams to delight customers. He is also a Mentor at Blackbird Ventures, where he helps startups with product strategy, design, and development. Simon hosts the Product Ops People Podcast, where he interviews guests about their work in product management and operations.

You can connect with me on:
🌐 https://www.simonhilton.co

Also by Alejandro Patterson & Simon Hilton

The Product Ops Pillars

Product Ops Pillars is the first book to provide an accessible summary of what modern Product Operations looks like. You'll learn how to improve your team's performance and efficiency, which tools are essential, and how to design an operating model that will keep your company on top.

The Product Culture Pyramid

"Product Culture Pyramid" is a insightful book that brings to light the pivotal role of product culture in the success of SaaS companies. Authored by an industry-leading expert, this book is designed to help you understand, build, and maintain a strong product culture that aligns with your business objectives.

Printed in Great Britain
by Amazon

39886403R00066